Save the Children

You're only young once… and what happens in those first few years shapes the rest of your life. *Save the Children* believes that every child should have the chance to grow up happy and healthy, and we are working with communities at home and overseas to help them to build a better future for their children.

Overseas *Save the Children* has major schemes in thirty countries, working to meet local needs. That means improving clinic services in Nepal, co-operating in Uganda's national immunisation programme, training community health workers in Bangladesh, helping handicapped children in Morocco and street children in Jamaica, and bringing clean water to villages in Honduras.

When disaster strikes, whether it's famine, flood, earthquake or hurricane, *SCF* is ready with immediate help. And *Save the Children* teams don't leave once the emergency is over; they stay on to help people to rebuild their lives.

SCF has over a hundred projects in Britain. Work is concentrated in the inner cities, where many children get off to an unfair start in life as they suffer the effects of poverty, unemployment and poor housing. As well as self-help family centres, *Save the Children* runs programmes for teenagers, schemes to help disabled children to get the most out of life, and a centre that gives many families their first ever holiday. There's support for homeless families, too.

Wherever *SCF* operates, their aim is the same: to develop programmes that will benefit tomorrow's children as well as today's.

Save the Children Fund · 17 Grove Lane · London SE5 8RD

KU-201-484

Illustrated by Peter Stevenson

Ladybird Books

Design by Graham Marlow; hand lettering by Marjory Purves.

British Library Cataloguing in Publication Data
Jokes, jokes, jokes.
   1. Jokes in English, 1945- —Anthologies—For children
   I. Stevenson, Peter   II. Series
   828′.91402′0809282
   ISBN 0-7214-1231-9

Published by Ladybird Books Ltd Loughborough Leicestershire UK
Ladybird Books Inc Auburn Maine 04210 USA
Printed in England

Foreword by
HRH The Princess Royal
President of
Save the Children

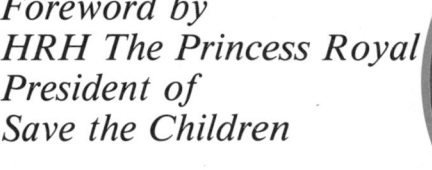

Laughter is one of the most precious gifts we can give and it plays a central role in everyone's childhood years.

There are, sadly, many children in the world who lack even basic conditions of life which we take for granted, such as health care, clean water and sufficient food.

It is highly appropriate therefore that the royalties from this delightful book will be going to help The Save the Children Fund continue their valuable work in these areas.

As President of the Fund, I should like to thank Ladybird Books for this, their second joke book in aid of Save the Children Fund, and the children at schools across the UK who kindly contributed their favourite jokes.

Anne

How did the frog cross the road?
He used the green cross toad.

What's the difference between a nail and a bad boxer?
One gets knocked in, the other gets knocked out!

Why did the crab go to jail?
Because he kept pinching things.

What do you get if you cross a sheep with a radiator?
Central bleating.

Why can't a car play football?
Because it's only got one boot.

What did one ear say to the other ear?
Between you and me we have brains

What happened to
the girl who slept
with her head under
the pillow?

*The fairies took
all her teeth away!*

What walks on its head all day?
A drawing pin stuck in your shoe.

Where do ghosts go swimming?
The Dead Sea.

Once upon a time there were three bears who made some porridge. While the porridge was cooling the bears went for a walk. When they came back Baby Bear said, "Who's been eating my porridge?" and Mummy Bear said, "Who's been eating my porridge?" and Daddy Bear said, "Never mind the porridge, where's the video gone?"

What do romantic owls
sing when it's
raining hard?
Too wet to woo.

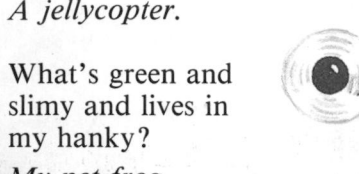

Can a match box?
No, but a tin can!

What goes up and wobbles?
A jellycopter.

What's green and
slimy and lives in
my hanky?
My pet frog.

Where do tadpoles
change into frogs?
In the croakroom!

What do you get if you cross a centipede with a
parrot?

A walkie talkie.

What is the difference between a buffalo and a bison?
You can't wash your hands in a buffalo.

Why is Cinderella bad at football?
Because she has a pumpkin for a coach.

What animals on Noah's ark didn't come in pairs?
Worms, they came in apples!

What do you get if you cross an elephant with a hose? A jumbo jet.

How can you tell if there is an elephant in the fridge?
The door won't close.

Why can't two elephants go swimming together?
Because they only have one pair of trunks.

ELEPHANT JOKES

Why do elephants wear green felt hats?
So that they can walk across snooker tables without being seen.

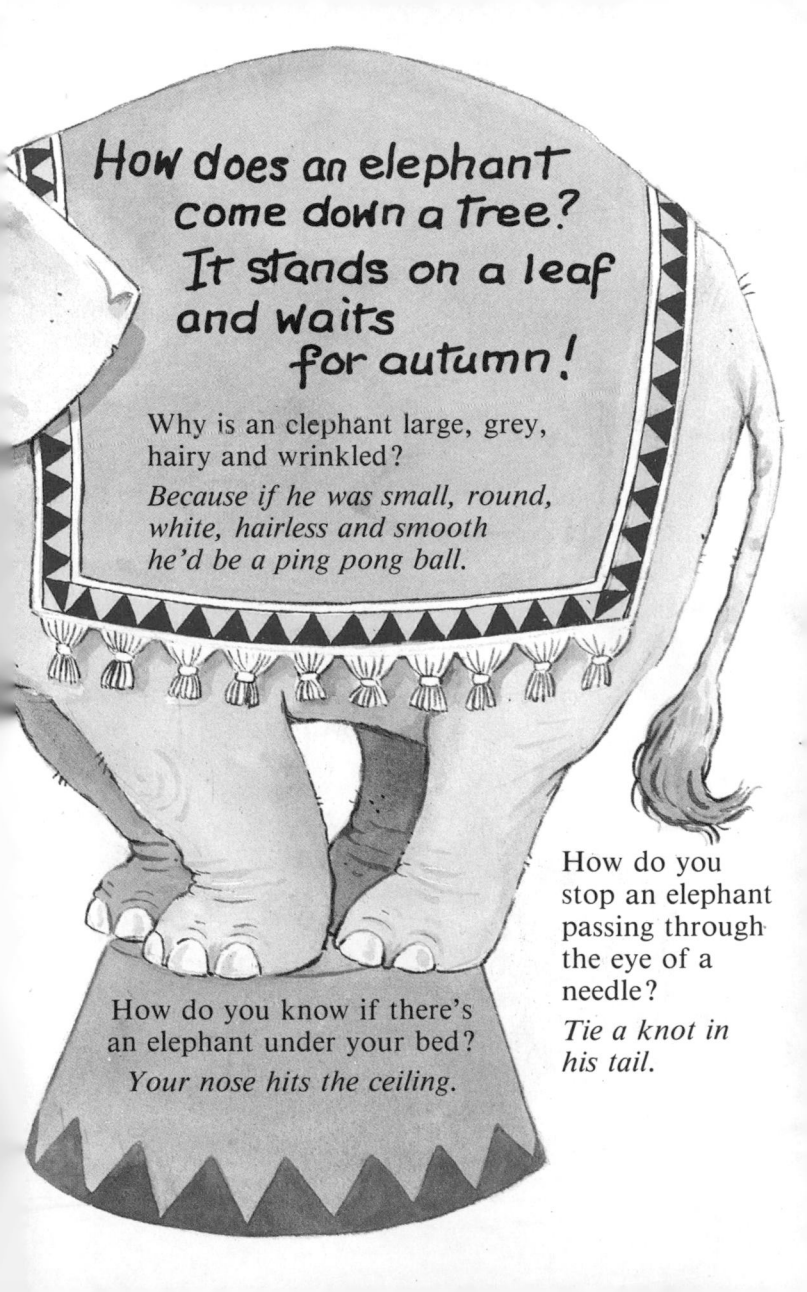

How does an elephant come down a tree? It stands on a leaf and waits for autumn!

Why is an elephant large, grey, hairy and wrinkled?

Because if he was small, round, white, hairless and smooth he'd be a ping pong ball.

How do you stop an elephant passing through the eye of a needle?

Tie a knot in his tail.

How do you know if there's an elephant under your bed?

Your nose hits the ceiling.

Where is Hadrian's wall?
In front of Hadrian's house.

What do you serve and don't eat?
Tennis balls.

What was Batman doing up the tree?
Looking for Robin's nest.

Daddy, Daddy, there's a spider in the bath.
Don't worry, you've seen a spider before.
Yes, but this one's four feet wide and it's using all the bath water.

How do you talk with fish?
Drop them a line.

Why did the robber
have a bath before he
robbed the bank?
He wanted a clean getaway.

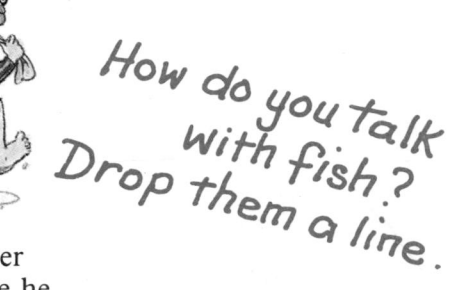

What are pilots'
favourite biscuits?
Plain biscuits.

If a blue house is made out of blue bricks,
and a yellow house is made out of yellow bricks,
and a red house is made out of red bricks, what is a
green house made out of?
Glass.

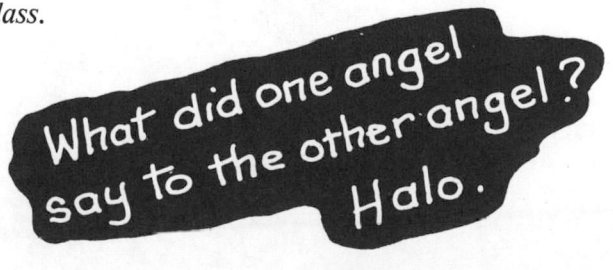

What did one angel
say to the other angel?
Halo.

HORSE JOKES

What always follows a horse?

It's tail.

Where do horses go when they are sick?

Horspital.

What has six legs and two heads?

A horse and rider.

How do you hire a horse?

Put four bricks under it.

What did the pony say when he coughed?

"Excuse me, I'm a little hoarse."

My new horse is very polite. Every time he comes to a jump he stops and lets me go first.

What did the driver say when he saw a biscuit being run over?
O Crumbs.

Why is it easy to weigh fish?
Because they have their own scales.

Why do bees buzz?
Because they can't whistle.

A lorry full of hairdriers was hijacked yesterday. Police are now combing the area.

Where does a whale sleep?
On the sea bed.

How do you start a jelly race?
Get set!

What kind of animal are you in the bath?
A bear.

JUNGLE

What is Tarzan's favourite Christmas song?
Jungle Bells.

Why do giraffes have long necks?
To connect their heads to their bodies.

What animal has the highest intelligence?
A giraffe.

How do you catch a monkey?
Hang upside down in a tree and make a noise like a banana.

Where does Tarzan get his clothes from?
A jungle sale.

What should you do if you find a gorilla asleep in your bed?
Sleep somewhere else.

JOKES

What did the lion say when he saw two hunters in a jeep?
Meals on wheels.

What's yellow and jumps from cake to cake?
Tarzipan.

What is black and white and has sixteen wheels?
A zebra on roller skates.

Customer: How do I know this crocodile purse is genuine?
Shopkeeper: By the way it snaps when it opens and shuts.

What do hippopotamuses have that no other animals have?

Little hippopotamuses.

There were two lions in a safari park watching families in their cars. One said to the other: "Isn't that cruel, caging people up like that!"

What happened to the snake with a cold?

She adder viper nose.

What does a little snake learn when it first goes to school?

Hiss-tory.

What animal can jump higher than a house?

They all can — a house can't jump!

Why did the tiger cross the road? Because it was th chicken's day of

There were two bloodthirsty bats. One went out and came back with blood all over his face.

1st bat: Where did you get all that blood from?
2nd bat: See that tree?
1st bat: Yes.
2nd bat: Well, I didn't!

What is the fastest vegetable?
A runner bean.

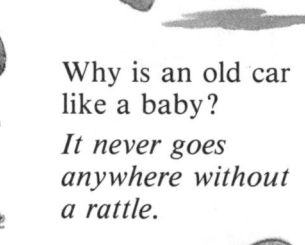

Why is an old car like a baby?
It never goes anywhere without a rattle.

What do you get if you cross a snowball with a shark? Frostbite.

What is badtempered and goes with custard?
Apple Grumble.

What's black and white and a bit red?
A penguin with nappy rash.

COW JOKES

What is the quickest way to count cows?
Use a cow-culator.

Why is milk the fastest thing on Earth?
It's pasteurised before you see it.

What is white, has just one horn and gives milk?
A milk van.

What do you get if you cross a cow and a jumping bean?
A milk shake.

What do cows do for entertainment?
Go to the moovies.

Why did the tap dancer have to retire?

He kept falling in the sink.

What has a bottom at the top? A leg.

What's brown, hairy, has no legs but walks?

Dad's socks.

What do bees do with all their honey?

They cell it.

What makes the Tower of Pisa lean?

It doesn't eat.

Why does the golfer always take a spare pair of trousers with him?

In case he gets a hole in one.

Which tree would you make a deck chair from? A beech tree.

Jimmy: Dad, what has a purple spotted body, ten hairy legs and big eyes on stalks?
Dad: I don't know, why?
Jimmy: One's just crawled up your trouser leg.

Mother: Have you given the goldfish fresh water today?

Lisa: No, they haven't finished the water I gave them yesterday.

How do you keep cool at a football match? Sit next to a fan.

Harry: When I sat down to play the piano, everyone laughed at me.

Mum: Why?

Harry: Because there wasn't a chair.

What is big, red and airy?
A red bus with its windows open.

What did one doorknob say to the other?
Don't fly off the handle.

Why is Sunday the strongest day
Because all the others
are weak days.

What lives underwater and carries lots of people? An octobus.

How did Noah manage in the dark?
He turned on the floodlights.

What did the pen say to the paper?
I dot my eyes on you.

"Jelly for Tea" by Eileen Joyit.

"Bell Ringing" by Paula Rope.

"Popular Songs" by Mel O'Dee.

"Tea for Two" by Roland Butta.

"All About Explosives" by Dinah Mite.

"Help for a Jail Breaker" by Freda Prisner.

"Sahara Journey," by I. Rhoda Camel.

What is small and
yellow and wears a
mask?
The Lone Lemon.

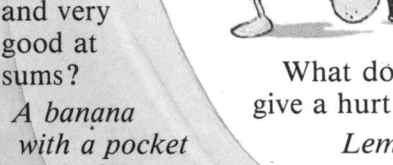

What is
yellow
and very
good at
sums?
*A banana
with a pocket
calculator.*

What do you
give a hurt lemon?
Lemonade.

What is yellow
and writes under water?
A ballpoint banana.

Why did the banana go out with the prune?
He couldn't find a date.

What's green,
hairy and wears
sunglasses?
A gooseberry on holiday.

What did one strawberry
say to another?
*"Your freshness got us
into this jam."*

What's a monster's
favourite soup?
Scream of tomato.

What's brown, wrinkled,
and glowing?
An electric prune.

What do thieves eat for lunch?
Beefburglars.

Diner: Is there soup on the menu?
Waiter: No, sir, I wiped it off.

What's green and
white and bounces?
A spring onion.

Mother: Sam, stop reaching across
the table. Haven't you got a tongue?
Sam: Yes, but my arm is longer.

Why were the cricket team given
cigarette lighters?
Because they lost all their matches.

Diner: Waiter, your thumb is in my soup.
Waiter: That's okay, sir, it's not hot.

What do you get if you dial
512632696723269001?
A blister on your finger.

What's long and green and always
points to the north?
A magnetic cucumber.

What is small and feathery and goes phut-phut-phut?
An outboard budgie.

What colour is a shout?
Yell-oh.

What do you always see running along the streets in town?
Pavements.

Escaped prisoner: I'm free, I'm free.
Little boy: So what! I'm four.

What goes into the water pink and comes out blue?
A swimmer on a cold day.

What cars do hot dogs like driving?
Rolls.

Flo: I've been seeing spots before my eyes lately.
Glo: Have you seen a doctor?
Flo: No, just spots.

How can you stop a fish from smelling?
Cut off its nose.

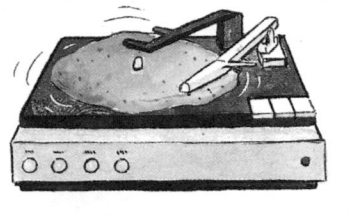

What is fat, yellow and goes round at 33⅓ r.p.m.?
A long playing omelette.

Two flies were sitting on Robinson Crusoe's knee. One fly said to the other: "It's getting hot around here – I'm off. I'll see you on Friday."

What do you get if you feed a chicken on whisky?
Scotch eggs.

The Thunder God went for a ride,
Upon his favourite filly.
"I'm Thor!" he cried.
The horse replied,
"You forgot your thaddle, thilly."

Why did little Bo-peep lose her sheep?
Because she had a crook with her.

CAT JOKES

Why did the kitten join the Red Cross?
He wanted to become a first aid kit.

Why does a cat purr?
For a purr-puss (purpose).

What do cats read?
The Mews of the World.

What works in a circus and meows when it swings?
An acrocat

What's grey with a blue face?
A mouse holding its breath.

Jim: I'm homesick.
Paul: But don't you live at home?
Jim: Yes, that's why I'm sick of it.

Mum: Have you filled the salt cellar yet?
Boy: No, it's hard work pushing all the salt through that little hole!

Peter: Why are you jumping up and down?
Jim: I took some medicine but forgot to shake the bottle.

Paul: My dad can hold up a car with one hand.
Jeremy: He must be really strong!
Paul: Oh no. He's a policeman!

What did one eye say to the other eye? Something's come between us that smells.

What do jelly babies wear on their feet
Gumboots.

Customer: Waiter, waiter, there's a twig in my soup!

Waiter: Yes, I know, sir. We have branches everywhere.

Customer: Waiter, waiter, there's a button in my salad.

Waiter: It must have fallen off your jacket potato, sir.

What's a hedgehog's favourite food.
Prickled onions.

What's a frog's favourite sweet?
Lollihop.

Why do Bank Managers carry briefcases?
Because briefcases don't walk.

What do disc jockeys wear?
Tracksuits.

Mum: Eat your cabbage, it'll put colour in your cheeks.
Boy: But I don't want green cheeks.

On which side does a chicken have the most feathers?
The outside.

What goes Tick-tick-woof-woof?
A watchdog.

I wonder where fleas go in winter?

Search me.

When you lose something, why do you always find it in the last place you look?
Because you always stop looking when you find it.

What is white and flies upwards?
A stupid snowflake

Knock, knock.
Who's there?
Mandy.
Mandy who?
Mandy lifeboats,
we're sinking.

Knock, knock!
Who's there?
Walrus.
Walrus who?
Why do you
walrus ask that
silly question?

Knock, knock.
Who's there?
Howard.
Howard who?
Howard you like to sit out here in the cold
while some idiot keeps on saying who's there?

Knock, knock.
Who's there?
Francis.
Francis who?
France's on the
other side of
the Channel.

Knock, knock.
Who's there?
Des.
Des who?
Des no door bell,
that's why I'm
knocking.

Knock, knock.
Who's there?
Phyllis.
Phyllis who?
Phyllis a glass
of water, I'm
thirsty.

Knock, knock.
Who's there?
Scott.
Scott who?
Scott nothing
to do with you.

Knock, knock.
Who's there?
Wood.
Wood who?
Wood you
believe, I've
forgotten.

Knock, knock!
Who's there?
Lettuce.
Lettuce who?
Lettuce in,
will you?

Knock, knock.
Who's there?
A boy who
can't reach
the doorbell.

Knock, knock!
Who's there?
Snow.
Snow who?
Snow good
asking me,
I don't know!

Boy: Mum, can I go
out and play?
Mum: What, in those
clothes?
Boy: No – in the park.

Boy: Daddy, Daddy,
there's a man at the
door with a bill.
Father: Don't be daft,
son, it's probably a
duck in a bowler hat!

Baby snake: Mum, are we poisonous snakes?

Mother snake: No, why?

Baby snake: Good, because I just bit my lip.

What did the composer write in the bath? Soap operas.

Customer: Waiter, waiter, there's a spider playing football in my soup.

Waiter: Yes, sir, he'll be playing in the Cup tomorrow.

What do you call a musical insect
A humbug.

What do you get if you cross an angry goat with Mount Everest? A butter mountain.

Did you hear about the stupid ghost?
He climbed over walls!

What pan can't be used for frying?
Marzipan.

Boy: Sniff, sniff.
Lady: Do you have a handkerchief?
Boy: Sorry, I don't lend it to strangers.

Surgeon: I suppose I'd better get back to the operating theatre – it's just about opening time again.

What sort of people sit in swivel chairs?
High up swivel servants.

Which burn longer, candles on a boy's birthday cake, or those on a girl's birthday cake?
Neither. They both burn shorter.

What does a vampire take when he has a cold? Coffin drops.

Did you hear about the man who didn't clean his spectacles?
He gave people dirty looks!

School Jokes

Pupil: Would you tell somebody off for something they didn't do?

Teacher: No, of course I wouldn't.

Pupil: Well, I haven't done my homework.

Teacher: Order! Order!

Cheeky boy: A hamburger and french fries, miss!

Teacher: What's the shortest month of the year?

Boy: May – it's only got three letters.

Teacher: Spell mouse.
Girl: M O U S
Teacher: But what's at the end of it?
Girl: A tail?

What is the most popular answer to teachers' questions?
I don't know.
Correct.

What did the decimal parrot say?
Pieces of ten! Pieces of ten!

How do you make seven an even number?
Take the 's' off.

If you had 50p in one pocket and 20p in the other, what would you have?
Someone else's trousers on, sir.

How did Newton discover the law of gravity?
By sheer apple-ication.

Teacher: That's a pretty little pet. What do you call him?
Boy: Tiny.
Teacher: Why?
Boy: Because he's my newt.

THE LIFE OF NEWTON

Teacher: John, why are you late?
John: I overslept, sir.
Teacher: You mean you sleep at home as well?

Why is the Tate Gallery like Scotland Yard? Because it's full of Constables.

"Mummy, am I really a polar bear?" asked the baby polar bear.

"Yes, of course, why?"

"Because I'm freezing!"

Boy: There's a man at the door collecting for the new swimming pool.

Dad: Give him a glass of water.

These potatoes have got specks on them.

Yes...that's because their eyes are shortsighted.

Why are snooker players patient? Because they don't mind standing at the end of a cue.

Did you hear about the boy who ran away with a circus?

The policeman made him bring it back.

Nervous driver to his instructor:
Take the wheel, please.
There's a tree heading for us.

Did you go waterskiing on holiday?
No. I couldn't find a lake with a slope.

Jim: My father owns a newspaper.
Paul: He must be rich.
Jim: Not really –
he bought it from a stall
this morning.

A man who was travelling
at 200 kilometres an hour
was stopped by the police.

*Sorry, was I driving
too fast?*

No, sir, flying too low.

What's the difference
between unlawful
and illegal?

*One's against the law
and the other's a sick
bird.*

Boy: Dad, have you got holes in your socks?
Dad: Certainly not!
Boy: Then how do you put your feet in?

DOCTOR DOCTOR

Patient: Doctor, doctor, everyone thinks I'm a cricket ball.
Doctor: How's that?
Patient: Oh, not you as well.

Doctor, Doctor, I can't stop stealing things.
I'll give you something to take.

Doctor, doctor, my eyesight is going!
I'm sorry, sir, this is the post office.

Doctor, Doctor, I've swallowed my camera.
Let's hope nothing develops.

What did one tonsil say to the other Tonsil? Get dressed, the doctor is taking us out Tonight.

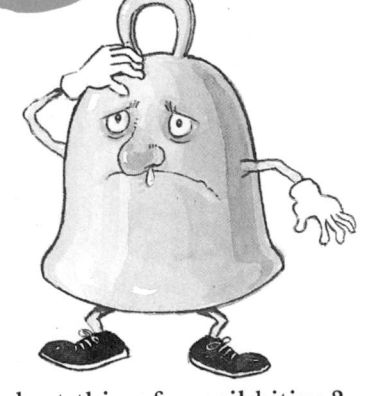

Doctor, doctor,
I feel like a bell.
*Well, take these,
and if they don't work
give me a ring.*

Doctor, doctor, what's the best thing for nail biting?
Sharp teeth!

Doctor, doctor, everyone keeps ignoring me.
Next please.

Why did the
egg stop rolling?
*It was out of
Shell.*

Why did six planks stand
in a circle?
To hold a board meeting.

What would you get if
you crossed a sheepdog
with a jelly?
Collie wobbles!

Where do
policemen live?
Letsby Avenue.

Brother: You just backed the car
over my bike!
Sister: Serves you right, you
shouldn't leave it in the hall.

1st Sailor: Why have you got that seagull on a lead?
2nd Sailor: I'm going to take a tern round the deck.

Which members of the orchestra can't you trust?
The fiddlers.

What is the best year for a kangaroo? A leap year!

1st boy: Did you hear that the next space shot is to the sun?
2nd boy: Won't they get burned?
1st boy: Of course not, silly! They're going at night.

My dog's bone idle.
Is he?
Last week I was watering the garden and he wouldn't lift a leg to help me.

What lies at the bottom of the sea and trembles?
A nervous wreck.

Why do bees hum? Because they don't know the words.

HHHUUUMMM

What do you call a
laughing hippo?
A happypotamus.

What do you call a
boy who likes fishing?
Rod.

What do you call a
small crab?
A little nipper.

What do you call an
idle flower?
A lazy daisy.

What do you call a
dinosaur with one eye?
Doyouthinkhesorus.

What do you call a
deer with no eyes?
No idea.

What do you call a
duck that robs safes?
A safe quacker.

What do you call a
soft-hearted, neat,
handsome monster?
A failure.

What do you call a
homeless snail?
A slug.

What do you call a
secret agent who lives in a
bottle of washing-up liquid?
Bubble 07.

Ladybird would like to thank the following schools for their help in making this book possible:

Carcroft First School, Carcroft, Doncaster
Chuckery Junior School, Walsall, West Midlands
Churchill C of E Primary School, Westerham, Kent
Contin Primary School, Contin, Strathpeffer
Dronfield Junior School, Dronfield, Sheffield
Gelli Crug Infants School, Abertillery, Gwent
Heighington Primary School, Heighington, Co Durham

MY PENCIL CASE